TRIPLE

BY ADAM STONE

BELLWETHER MEDIA · MINNEAPOLIS, MN

JB
T835

Are you ready to take it to the extreme?
Torque books thrust you into the action-packed world
of sports, vehicles, mystery, and adventure. These books
may include dirt, smoke, fire, and dangerous stunts.
WARNING: read at your own risk.

Library of Congress Cataloging-in-Publication Data

Stone, Adam.
  Triple H / by Adam Stone.
     p. cm. -- (Torque: pro wrestling champions)
  Includes bibliographical references and index.
  Summary: "Engaging images accompany information about Triple H. The combination of high-interest
subject matter and light text is intended for students in grades 3 through 7"--Provided by publisher.
  ISBN 978-1-60014-641-1 (hardcover : alk. paper)
  1. Triple H., 1969---Juvenile literature. 2. Wrestlers--United States--Biography--Juvenile literature. I.
Title.
  GV1196.T75S76 2011
  796.812092--dc22
  [B]   2011012232

This edition first published in 2012 by Bellwether Media, Inc.

Printed in the United States of America, North Mankato, MN.

080111   1187

CONTENTS

NO WAY OUT

It was No Way Out 2008. Triple H stared down five other wrestlers in the ring. He was in an **Elimination Chamber Match** against Shawn Michaels, Jeff Hardy, Chris Jericho, John "Bradshaw" Layfield, and Umaga. All six wrestlers were inside a steel chamber. The winner would earn a shot at the World Wrestling Entertainment (WWE) Championship.

VITAL STATS

Wrestling Name: _____ Triple H

Real Name: _____ Paul Michael Levesque

Height: _____ 6 feet, 4 inches (1.9 meters)

Weight: _____ 255 pounds (116 kilograms)

Started Wrestling: _____ 1992

Finishing Move: _____ Pedigree

Eventually, only Triple H and Hardy remained. Triple H grabbed Hardy and did a **Pedigree**. The move drove Hardy's head into a metal chair. Triple H went for the pin. The referee counted to three. Triple H had won his shot at the championship!

QUICK HIT!

Triple H is an Elimination Chamber Match specialist. He has won four of these tough matches over his career.

WHO IS TRIPLE H?

Triple H's real name is Paul Michael Levesque. He was born on July 27, 1969 in Nashua, New Hampshire. Young Levesque was a big wrestling fan. His favorite wrestler was Ric Flair.

Levesque was a skinny kid until early high school. At age 14, he got a free membership at a gym. He began to spend a lot of time lifting weights.

Levesque graduated from high school in 1987. He was 210 pounds (95 kilograms) of pure muscle. He won several **bodybuilding** competitions. However, Levesque did not want to be a professional bodybuilder. He wanted to be a wrestler.

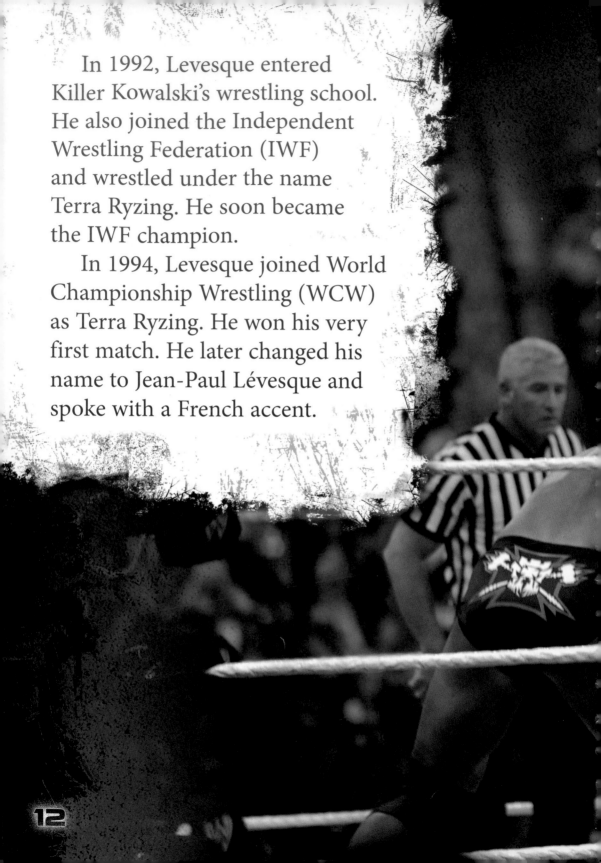

In 1992, Levesque entered Killer Kowalski's wrestling school. He also joined the Independent Wrestling Federation (IWF) and wrestled under the name Terra Ryzing. He soon became the IWF champion.

In 1994, Levesque joined World Championship Wrestling (WCW) as Terra Ryzing. He won his very first match. He later changed his name to Jean-Paul Lévesque and spoke with a French accent.

BECOMING A CHAMPION

In 1995, Levesque joined WWE. His name was "Connecticut Blueblood" Hunter Hearst Helmsley. That name was soon changed to Triple H. He started out as a **heel**. He went back and forth between being a heel and a **face** over the next few years.

QUICK HIT!

Triple H pinned Mankind to win his first WWE Championship in 1999.

Triple H is a WWE fan favorite. His **technique** and aggressive style have helped him win many championships. His nickname is "The Game" because he is always on top of his game.

Triple H's wrestling style has led to a few injuries. He hurt his left leg in 2001 and his right leg in 2007. He made a comeback both times.

HIGH
KNEE
STRIKE

Many of Triple H's **signature moves** require a lot of strength. He picks up his opponent to perform a spinebuster. He throws the opponent to the mat and lands on top of him. His high knee strike is another powerful move. He runs toward an opponent and leaps into the air. He raises his knee and hits the opponent in the head.

The Pedigree is Triple H's **finishing move**. Triple H usually performs it before going for a pin. Triple H puts his opponent's head between his legs. Then he jumps and bends his knees. The opponent's head slams into the mat as Triple H lands on it. Triple H is always on his game with the help of this destructive move.

GLOSSARY

bodybuilding—lifting weights to build up a lot of muscle

Elimination Chamber Match—a match in which six wrestlers are locked in a steel chamber; the last wrestler standing is the winner.

face—a wrestler seen by fans as a hero

finishing move—a wrestling move meant to finish off an opponent so that he can be pinned

heel—a wrestler seen by fans as a villain

Pedigree—Triple H's finishing move; Triple H puts the opponent's head between his legs and then jumps and bends his knees, smashing the opponent's face into the mat.

signature moves—moves that a wrestler is famous for performing

technique—skillful and proper performance of moves

TO LEARN MORE

AT THE LIBRARY

Black, Jake. *The Ultimate Guide to WWE.* New York,
N.Y.: Grosset & Dunlap, 2010.

Kaelberer, Angie Peterson. *Triple H.* Mankato, Minn.:
Capstone Press, 2010.

Shields, Brian. *Triple H.* New York, N.Y.: DK
Publishing, 2009.

ON THE WEB

Learning more about
Triple H is as easy as 1, 2, 3.

1. Go to www.factsurfer.com.

2. Enter "Triple H" into the search box.

3. Click the "Surf" button and you will see a list of
related Web sites.

With factsurfer.com, finding more information
is just a click away.

INDEX